Toxins in the Food Chain

Sarah Levete

CRABTREE
Publishing Company
www.crabtreebooks.com

Crabtree Publishing Company
www.crabtreebooks.com

Author:
Sarah Levete

Editorial director:
Kathy Middleton

Proofreaders:
Crystal Sikkens, Molly Aloian

Designer:
Paul Myerscough

Production coordinator:
Kenneth Wright

Prepress technician:
Kenneth Wright

Illustrations:
Geoff Ward

Cover:
Giving growth hormones to cattle may produce more meat, but how does it affect the people who eat it?

Photos:
Alamy Images: Tengku Mohd Yusof p. 9b; Corbis: Desmond Boyland/Reuters p. 20, China Daily/Reuters p. 15, Jane Hahn/EPA p. 25, Chris Rainier p. 17b, Bob Sacha p. 17t, George Steinmetz p. 21b; Fotolia: Indigo p. 26, Look Photo p. 11t; Istockphoto: Nick Belton p. 8-9, Matthew Rambo p. 1, 3, 6, 6–7, 30–31, 32; Rex Features: Sipa Press p. 21t; Shutterstock: Cathleen Abers-Kimball p. 13, Vera Bogaerts p. 10-11, Joy Brown p. 29b, Fernando Blanco Calzada p. 24t, Paul Cowan p. 23b, Countryroad p. 29t, Jose Gill p. 23t, Iofoto p. 19, Italianestro p. 24-25, Patsy A. Jacks p. 16-17, Renars Jurkovskis p. 12, Kameel4u p. 14, Sergey Kamshylin p. 4–5, Susanne Krogh-Hansen p. 11b, Kuzma p. 22, Zacarias Pereira da Mata p. 20–21, Lilac Mountain p. 9t, Gillian Mowbray p. 4, Mrfotos p. 18-19, Antonio Jorge Nunes p. 27t, Alistair Scott p. 26-27, Semenovp p. 28-29, Alexander Studentschnig p. 14–15.

Cover Photograph:
Corbis: (Stephen Frank)

Library and Archives Canada Cataloguing in Publication

Levete, Sarah
        Toxins in the food chain / Sarah Levete.

(Protecting our planet)
Includes index.
ISBN 978-0-7787-5215-8 (bound).--ISBN 978-0-7787-5232-5 (pbk.)

        1. Food contamination--Juvenile literature. 2. Food--Toxicology--
Juvenile literature. 3. Food chains (Ecology)--Juvenile literature.
I. Title. II. Series: Protecting our planet (St. Catharines, Ont.)

RA1258.L49 2010   j363.19'2   C2009-905263-6

Library of Congress Cataloging-in-Publication Data

Levete, Sarah.
Toxins in the food chain / Sarah Levete.
        p. cm. -- (Protecting our planet)
Includes index.
ISBN 978-0-7787-5232-5 (pbk. : alk. paper)
-- ISBN 978-0-7787-5215-8 (reinforced library binding : alk. paper)
1. Food--Toxicology--Juvenile literature. I. Title. II. Series.

RA1258.L48 2010
615.9'54--dc22

                                        2009034883

Crabtree Publishing Company
www.crabtreebooks.com   1-800-387-7650

Published in Canada
Crabtree Publishing
616 Welland Ave.
St. Catharines, ON
L2M 5V6

Published in the United States
Crabtree Publishing
PMB16A
350 Fifth Ave., 59th floor
New York, NY 10118

Printed in China/122009/CT20090915

Published by CRABTREE PUBLISHING COMPANY.
Copyright © **2010**

Contents

Passing on the poisons

Toxins are poisons. Many are found in nature and help protect plants, fungi, mosses, fish, **reptiles**, and **amphibians** against creatures that try to eat them. Toxins do this by causing a nasty reaction in the feeders' bodies. Without these toxins, many species would not survive.

Toxins in the food chain

We use natural toxins in very small amounts as medicines. We also enjoy others, such as caffeine, which we drink in tea and coffee. But there are other toxins that are very harmful, especially when they enter the food chain. Many of these are artificial chemicals. They can be taken up by plants, and then taken in by animals that eat the plants. This is how toxins rise through the food chain. They enter the food chain in many ways.

▼ *After the Chernobyl nuclear disaster in 1986, many sheep in Wales grazed on highly radioactive grass.*

CASE STUDY

The impact of Chernobyl

Some toxins enter the food chain because of a disaster. This is what happened at the Chernobyl nuclear power plant in the Ukraine on April 26, 1986. One of its reactors, where nuclear energy is made, exploded twice. Huge quantities of invisible and highly toxic **radioactive** substances shot into the air. These toxins can cause cancers and deformities, or disfigured parts, in plants, animals, and humans.

Radioactivity cannot be seen, but it can be detected. Within hours, 60 percent of the accident's **radioactive fallout** had hit the nearby country of Belarus. Within a few days, high, gusting winds had spread it westwards to Germany, Scandinavia, and the United Kingdom. In northern Scandinavia, the toxins were absorbed, or soaked in, easily from the air by plant-like **lichens**, which are eaten by reindeer. Reindeer herders were forced to kill many of their livestock. Sheep farmers in Wales could not sell their sheep, which fed on grass with high levels of radioactivity. Scientific tests are still carried out on the grass in this area today.

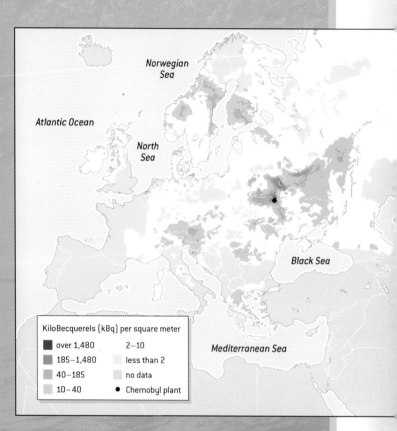

KiloBecquerels (kBq) per square meter

- ■ over 1,480
- ■ 185–1,480
- ■ 40–185
- ■ 10–40
- □ 2–10
- □ less than 2
- □ no data
- ● Chernobyl plant

▲ *This map shows the amount of radioactive fallout, measured in KiloBecquerels, over Europe as a result of the Chernobyl disaster.*

For miles around Chernobyl, radioactive substances sank into soils where crops were grown. They seeped into **groundwater**, which humans draw up to drink. They were washed into streams where fish swam. Today, radioactive fallout from Chernobyl is still in the food chain. Several thousand people from the area will die early because of cancer or other illnesses caused by the radioactivity.

What is a food chain?

Toxins can enter one environment and spread to others by the wind. Or they can wash into **waterways**. They can soak down, or **leach** into soils. Toxins can leach right down into groundwater. These different ways of spreading toxins mean that a wide range of plants and animals can be affected. Animals can drink contaminated, or poisoned, water and they can eat food that contains the toxin.

Chain of energy

In any environment, there are a lot of different food chains. Each food chain allows energy to pass from plants to different animals. The Sun's energy begins the chain. The green parts of plants, **algae**, and some bacteria use energy from the Sun to create food energy. This, together with water and **nutrients**, helps them to grow. Some energy is stored in plants' leaves, seeds, and fruits. These are then eaten by creatures that use the stored energy to help them grow and reproduce.

◄ *Discarded engine oil is a hazard. It can quickly contaminate and pollute our vital water supplies.*

An insect might eat a leaf, a bird might eat the insect, and a wild cat might eat the bird. The energy has been passed through the links in the chain. When a plant or animal takes in toxins, these can be passed up the food chain, too. The wild cat is at the top of its food chain. It needs to eat a lot of small birds and mammals to survive. It can therefore eat a lot of toxins, too.

Tangled web

There are not usually more than about four links in each food chain. But there are often many different creatures that eat a particular food. For instance, birds eat insects, but so do shrews. Wild cats eat birds and shrews, so they could take in toxins from both. All these simple food chains link together in a complicated way to form what is called a food web.

The energy chain ends when a living thing dies. It is then broken down by bacteria and fungi into nutrients. These go back into the soil and help plants to grow. Then the chain begins again.

Fact bank

Links in the chain:

- Producers in the food chain make food. Plants are producers.

- Consumers eat producers or other consumers. Deer eat leaves, and wolves eat the deer. Both are consumers.

- Decomposers break down dead plant and animal matter. There are over 100,000 different decomposers, such as bacteria.

- Decomposed material helps nourish plants, which are producers.

▼ *This diagram shows a food chain. Toxins can pass all the way up a food chain, from the plants at the bottom of the chain to the animals at the top.*

grasshopper eats grass

mouse eats grasshopper

bird eats mouse

Algal blooms

Algae are simple plant-like forms that live in or on water. In the sea, they are food for tiny creatures called zooplankton, which in turn are eaten by fish and even some whales. Some algae suddenly appear in vast, colorful masses on the water. These are algal blooms, and some can be toxic to the food chain.

Overfed algae

Toxic blooms are caused mostly by sewage and fertilizers. These contain nitrogen and phosphate chemicals. In farming, fertilizers help crops to grow. But when too many fertilizer chemicals wash into ponds, lakes, streams, and rivers they cause algae to grow and multiply too quickly.

Blankets of algae cover ponds, lakes, and slow-moving streams. They stop light from reaching the plants beneath. They also use up oxygen in the water. Oxygen keeps the animals that live in the water alive, healthy, and able to breed. The water itself goes stale and water plants begin to decay, which in turn poisons fish and other creatures.

▼ *Algae is a hazard when it becomes out of control. It can swamp areas of water and suffocate plant and animal life.*

Poisonous seas

On our seas, tides of algal blooms can look spectacular. But some algae can poison the food chain. Humans can become very ill if they eat shellfish that have taken in toxins from these algae. The toxins can cause two main illnesses: Paralytic Shell Poisoning, which causes paralysis, or loss of movement in the body, and Amnesic Shell Poisoning, which causes amnesia, or loss of memory, or even death. These poisonous algal blooms appear as "red tides."

▲ *If an excess of algae starves fish of oxygen in the water, they can die.*

"It (algae) occurs all over the place in all kinds of water bodies and when conditions are right, when it's calm and there's lots of nutrients, then it takes advantage and grows."

Jonathon Shadwell, UK Environment Agency, June 2005

WHAT CAN BE DONE?

In 1991, Australia was hit by the world's longest toxic freshwater algal bloom. It sprang up along the Barron and Darling rivers in New South Wales. The New South Wales government had to do something and has since reduced the use of fertilizers. It has planned better ways of getting rid of sewage. Riverbank erosion has been stopped, too. This prevents fertilized soil from crumbling into rivers. Dam waters are "stirred" by releasing waters in small spurts, which prevents algae from forming.

Algae is a familiar sight on the ➤ *surface of many waterways. This algae is growing too quickly.*

Chemicals and crops

The world needs to grow a lot of food for its 6.7 billion people. Farmers often struggle with weeds, fungi, and crop-eating pests—such as insects. Their answer is to spray on chemicals that spread into soil, waterways, groundwater and reach the sea. The chemicals then find their way into the food chain.

Harmful herbicides

Farmers use **hormones** as a **herbicide** to shrink the roots of weeds. **Fungicides** are used to stop fungi from growing on plants. However, these hormones are entering water systems close to agricultural land. In parts of the United States, hormone levels in these water habitats can be so high that they can change some species of male fish into female fish. This affects the mating habits of the fish and their ability to reproduce. Hormones in these fish are passed on to bigger fish that eat them—and on through the food chain.

▼ *Farmers spray crops with herbicides, fungicides, and pesticides to protect them from weeds, fungi, and insects.*

▲ *The pesticide this farmer is spraying on his crops will find its way into the food chain.*

WHAT CAN BE DONE? Many herbicides, pesticides, and fungicides are now being developed from natural toxins in some plant varieties. Because these are more natural, they are less likely to build up in the environment and pass up through food chains. Some of the new natural herbicides are made from the roots of the spotted knapweed plant and the leaves of the black walnut tree.

Deadly pesticides

Some farmers also use a powerful group of **pesticides**. They attack the nervous systems of insects. Through the food chain, they can do the same to humans. They can also cause birth defects. When plant matter is burned with traces of such pesticides, chemicals that cause cancers are created.

Many of the most toxic pesticides have been banned, but they still linger in the food chain. We do not know how long they will last. We also do not really understand the effects of spraying against insects, weeds, and fungi at the same time. It is thought that the build-up of this mix of chemicals could be responsible for killing bee colonies in Europe, the United States, and Canada.

Using chemicals in farming may produce better ➤ *crops, such as this rapeseed, but do we really know what effect the toxins have on our health?*

11

Toxins in meat

Livestock, such as cattle, are fed on grasses, food pellets, and chemicals. When we eat the animals' meat or drink their milk we take in some of the chemicals, too. They are passed on through the food chain.

More meaty

Many cattle raised for meat are injected with growth hormones. This makes their muscle mass bigger and produces more meat. In the United States, about two-thirds of cattle are given hormones. That's about 24 million cattle each year. At a cost of $1–$3 per animal, the hormone creates up to 20 percent extra meat. That's a lot of extra meat to sell.

▲ Growth hormone injections may give more meat, but what is the real cost?

WHAT CAN BE DONE?

Organic meat is one answer to the problem of toxins released into the food chain through animal rearing. Organically reared livestock are fed with 95 percent chemical-free grains, leaves, and grasses. The remaining 5 percent of animal feed can contain only chemicals approved by official government departments of agriculture. Organically reared animals are not injected with hormones or antibiotics, either. In these ways, organic meat is mainly chemical-free. The animals' droppings, do not add harmful chemicals to the soil or waterways.

Chemicals in our chickens

Most intensively reared chickens are bred to grow quickly. In many countries they are also given growth hormones to speed up the process. These chickens grow so fast they are ready to eat after just 38 days, rather than the normal 80 days. This gives the farmer a quick turnover and more profit.

Free-range chickens are allowed to ▶ roam, rather than being cooped up like intensively reared chickens.

These chickens are bred in huge sheds that contain many thousands of birds. The cramped living conditions lead to disease. Chicken farmers use antibiotics to prevent infection in their flocks. These antibiotics are passed on to humans through the food chain when we eat the meat. Many diseases that affect humans are now becoming resistant to antibiotics. This may be due to the increased levels of antibiotics in our diet. Our bodies simply get used to antibiotics and so do not respond to antibiotic treatments when we are sick.

From animals to water

Chemicals used in meat and milk production pass into the animals' droppings. This washes into water systems and leaches down into groundwater. Strong concentrations of chemicals have been found in waters close to cattle sheds, where there is a lot of dung.

Toxic cleaning products

Laundry detergents and cleaning products contain harmful chemicals that get washed down into soil and water systems. They are absorbed by algae in rivers, earthworms on land, and are eaten by tiny creatures in the sea, such as shelled **crustaceans**.

Too clean for the planet

Many cleaning products now contain chemicals that kill bacteria, called antibacterial. Antibacterial chemicals are found in everything from kitchen surface cleaners to deodorants.

However, these types of chemicals are killing bacteria that are helpful to our environment. Antibacterial chemicals also stop antibiotic medicines from working properly when bacteria infect people.

Detergents and ➤ chemicals found in cleaning products often end up as a frothy scum on rivers or beaches.

Antibacterials are difficult to clear from our sewage systems. In some countries, they are still present in sewage sludge that is spread over farmland. They are easily leached into waterways, too. About 58 percent of rivers and streams tested in the United States contain these chemicals.

Toxins in our detergents

Other cleaning products, such as **surfactants**, loosen grease and dirt from clothes. They are present in many laundry detergents. But they release benzene chemicals into the environment while they are being manufactured. These chemicals can trigger hormones in fish that change their mating behavior.

▲ *Dye from local factories is pouring into the Huanghe River in China. Many cleaning products and dyes are toxic to plants and animals, but they can still find their way into the food chain.*

CASE STUDY

Fashion and the food chain

The fashion for stone-washed jeans has led to toxins in the food chain. In Tehuacan, Mexico, many local clothes manufacturers use bleach and other chemicals in the stone-washing process. These very strong chemicals are washed into streams. Here, the bleach has burned aquatic plant roots and **sterilized** the soil. It has wiped out tiny insects and worms—the foundations of the food chain.

The bright blue waste-water trickles onto corn fields, too. Here, the dyes and chemicals have made the top soil crumbly, gray-blue, and full of toxins. Tehuacan was once famous for its mineral water but can no longer bottle it because it contains too many toxins from the jeans. The Tehuacan city council monitors the output from jeans makers. But many factories are being set up just outside the council's control, so the problem still continues.

Toxic air and water

Since the beginning of the Industrial Revolution over 200 years ago, factories have been polluting the food chain. Factories and power stations emit gases and chemicals held in water droplets through smokestacks. **Acids** are washed away in factory waste products. From here they enter all environments—from soils to the sea.

Gases enter the food chain

Some of the worst waste gases and gas combinations are carbon monoxide, sulphur dioxide, nitrogen oxide, hydrocarbons, and dioxins. Plant leaves can take these in through stomata, or holes, in their leaves. Birds and mammals can breathe them in. But their worst effects on the food chain happen through acid rain, when chemicals mix with water droplets in rainclouds.

Sulphur dioxide gas changes into sulphuric acid and becomes particularly toxic. It strips nutrients from the soil.

◄ *Factories, such as paper mills, can pollute both air and water.*

▲ *Toxic substances can drain quickly from streams and rivers, such as the Yangtze River in China above, into lakes, reservoirs, and seas.*

This acid stops trees from growing and breaks up tree bark, so that insects can bore inside the tree and kill it. Sulphuric acid also washes aluminium out of the soil. It then drains into lakes. Here, this highly toxic substance kills fish and other life forms at the bottom of the food chain.

Stopping the smoke

Many factories release particulates, which are tiny solid or liquid particles that are suspended, or held, in gases. They move through the air in the same way as smoke. They also find their way into the food chain. When humans breathe them in these tiny particles can cause lung cancer and heart disease.

> "...not only in the soil, but also the groundwater, vegetables and even breast milk is contaminated...by heavy metals like nickel, chromium, mercury and lead...."
>
> Dr. Amrit Nair, *Surviving Bhopal: Toxic Present, Toxic Future*, 2008

CASE STUDY

Toxic leak, Bhopal, India

In the Indian city of Bhopal on December 4, 1984, a huge chemical disaster occurred. A massive cloud of leaked gases ballooned above a pesticide factory. The pesticides used a particularly toxic chemical called carbaryl. The cocktail of toxic fumes that erupted on that day included carbon monoxide and hydrogen cyanide. Three thousand people were killed immediately, 8,000 over the following two weeks, and 8,000 more through sickness. Today, the chemicals are still found in the soils, crops, drinking water, fish, and milk of Bhopal.

▼ *Bhopal was the scene of the worst industrial accident in the world.*

17

Metals in the food chain

Metals are all around us and beneath our feet in rocks and soils. They have been entering the food chain since time began. Volcanic eruptions and mining have brought once buried metals to the surface. Some are harmless, but others are toxic to the food chain.

The price of gold

Mining is the greatest cause of metal poisoning. In many parts of the world gold is extracted, or taken out, by cyanide leaching. This is a chemical process that uses sodium or potassium cyanide to dissolve the gold from the rocks. If waste cyanide washes into streams, it is deadly poisonous to plants, animals, and people.

Miners suffer too from breathing in the cyanide. Another method of gold extraction uses mercury to bond with tiny pieces of gold, which helps separate the gold from the crushed rock that surrounds it. Mercury is also deadly poisonous to the food chain. It can be found in soils and water where this type of gold mining has occurred.

▼ *The toxic waste from an abandoned gold mine has poisoned this river.*

Old mines are still toxic

In old mines, bacteria act on exposed metals and break them down. This creates acids which burn plants, poison invertebrates, or animals without a backbone such as worms, and are washed into water systems.

When metals are mined, waste materials are often dumped nearby. These can often contain quantities of metals that are too small to be worth mining. But they still remain poisonous to animals. Scientists have found that growing a grass called alfalfa can help clean up these mining dumps. The alfalfa grass takes up the poisonous metals from the soil.

Monitoring metals

Algae easily absorb metal minerals and metal poisons such as arsenic. Many algae take in the metal zinc, which helps them to grow. Scientists have found that if zinc is scarce, algae will absorb another metal called cadmium as well. However, cadmium could prove extremely toxic in high doses to animals that eat the algae. Water fleas called Daphnia can also take in high concentrations of metal minerals. Algae and Daphnia are vital to the food chain, and scientists study both to monitor metal toxins.

▲ *Mineral waste from mines is often deposited in pools of water called tailing ponds. These pools of toxic waste can easily leach into the soil or spread into waterways.*

Fact bank

Metals and their toxic effects:

- Arsenic is a semi-metal that can kill in large doses.

- Cadmium is used in batteries and as coloring. It causes cancers and kidney damage.

- Lead is a soft metal found in old pipework and roofing. It builds up in the body and can damage the kidneys and the nervous and reproductive systems.

- Mercury is used in industry. It is absorbed through the skin and builds up in the body. Mercury affects the brain and can kill.

Oil and the food chain

Petroleum oil is a fossil fuel. It was formed millions of years ago from billions of tiny creatures. When they died they were laid down in a thick layer of mud. This was pressed and heated deep in Earth until it turned into oil. Petroleum oil is toxic to most plants and animals.

Oil's poisons

Oil contains acids and traces of metals. Many of these are harmful to living things. They can attack all points on the food chain. These toxic acids and metals can cause cancer in humans and harm reproduction even in large creatures such as whales. They stop tiny algae and shellfish from multiplying, too. The oily substance also prevents small creatures from breathing or taking in oxygen through gills or their skin.

▲ *Most animals cannot survive the damaging effects of an oil spill.*

In plants, roots are burned by acids and blocked by oil. The tiny holes in their leaves cannot take in oxygen, so the plants wither and die.

Oil enters the food chain through leaks when oil is extracted or from oil spills caused by tankers. When oil rigs or leaks in oil pipelines catch fire, the burning oil billows out dark, poisonous clouds. Acid rain can form inside these clouds.

▲ This clean-up operation in Brittany, France, took place after the Amoco Cadiz oil tanker ran aground there in 1978.

CASE STUDY

Oil on the Niger Delta

Nigeria's Niger Delta is a large oil-producing region. A delta is a low-lying area where a river meets the sea. Waters here are normally very calm, so spilled oil sits in pools along hundreds of winding creeks. Over the years toxins have poisoned millions of fish, and the humans who have eaten them. Toxins have burned the twisting mangrove plants that line the banks. But in Ogbogu District, scientists are now using plants to help clear up the oil. A highly absorbent leafy plant, *Hibiscus cannabinus*, is laid on top of the oily water. It soaks up the toxins through its leaves. The leaves are then taken away from the area and applied with microorganisms that safely break down the toxic hydrocarbons in the oil.

A grass called *Vitiveria zizanioides* is grown in some oil-polluted areas. Its fibrous roots can absorb toxins and remove them from the surrounding soil and water systems.

▼ Oil brings wealth to the Niger Delta, but the oil industry also causes pollution.

21

Plastics in the food chain

The main material used to make plastics is petroleum oil, which itself is toxic. But the most serious poisons in plastics are chemicals used to soften the plastic. It is these that harm the food chain—from algae to humans.

Poisons in plastics

Some of the most dangerous chemicals are found in soft, bendy plastics. Acids called phthalates make the plastics bendy. But some scientists are now linking them to breeding problems in fish, animals, and humans.

The most damaging type of plastic is pliable PVC. PVC production fuses, or joins, vinyl chloride with toxic metals, such as lead and cadmium. These stabilize and soften the substance to make many products, from shower curtains to soft toys and babies' teething rings.

Waste on a beach ➤ may not just be an eyesore—plastics can break down in saltwater and enter the food chain.

▲ *Plastic bags thrown into the sea are swallowed by whales and become trapped in their digestive systems. This can eventually kill them.*

There are many laws that regulate harmful chemicals in plastics but it is hard to enforce them. Many plastic manufacturers are now making safer plastics, such as polyethylene. But the best way of helping the food chain is to use less plastic, especially bags and bottles. It can take 450 years for a plastic bottle to break down completely.

PVC has been known to release mercury, which poisons organs such as the kidneys. PVC also releases cancer-causing dioxins when it is manufactured. It is thought that at least 295 million tons (300 million tonnes) of PVC have been made in the last 50 years.

▼ *If plastic garbage is thrown into the sea, some of it will wash up on beaches. The beaches then become polluted with toxic waste.*

Plastics forever?

Tiny particles called microplastics begin to wear off plastic waste, such as bottles. This happens particularly quickly in saltwater. Microplastics have been found to absorb other toxins in the water very easily. This makes their effect on the food chain even more dangerous. These very tiny toxic particles are swallowed by fish and eaten by whale species that normally feed on tiny plants and animals such as **plankton**.

23

Toxins in technology

Old, abandoned computers, televisions, washing machines, and many other electronic goods are known as e-waste. All e-waste contains toxins, from metals and plastics to acids and gases. Some are released when they are broken up. Other toxins are released when they are burned. But all affect the food chain.

E-waste in the food chain

Poisonous metals from e-waste are the biggest problem. Arsenic, barium, selenium, cadmium, lead, mercury, and chromium flame retardant which resist fire, are all highly toxic. Most of these affect the nervous system and vital organs, such as the liver and kidneys. Cadmium also causes anaemia in people, which is when the blood does not have enough iron in it. It can damage bones and make them thin, too. Fish, birds, mammals, and humans all suffer these effects by eating contaminated foods.

▲ There is a growing awareness that batteries are a source of environmental pollution.

◄ This thrown-away computer circuit boa is now e-waste. When it is destroyed, toxins from the chemicals it is made from may pass into the environment.

Dumping e-waste

Toxins from electronic goods build up on waste sites. Here, they leach into soils. In the United States, 30 million computers are dumped every year. Only 14 percent are properly recycled. In the United Kingdom, over 1 million tons (or tonnes) of e-waste end up in **landfill sites**. Many old, banned substances are found on these sites, such as cancer-causing **PCBs**.

These were once used as insulators in electrical equipment but are very dangerous because they keep building up in the soil.

> *"The world's richest nations are dumping hazardous electronic waste on poor African countries."*
>
> **Achim Steiner, head of United Nations Environment Program (UNEP), 2006**

CASE STUDY

E-waste dumping in Ghana

Many rich countries send their unwanted computers and other e-waste to poorer countries that lack funds for computer equipment. Ghana has huge e-waste sites. Like most poorer countries, they have no proper disposal units for breaking down computer parts without polluting the environment.

Many people in Ghana live on $2 U.S. a day. Collecting metals, such as copper, from old computers can bring in $5 U.S. for a small bundle. This is why people accept e-waste dumping, but it is a huge environmental problem for Ghana.

▼ *E-waste dumped on a site in Ghana. More computers need to be recycled properly.*

Poisons past and future

Toxins can stay in the food chain for many years. They can build up in the fatty tissue of animals. Many toxins, such as arsenic and cadmium, stay in the body forever. Some substances, such as metals from mines, are not toxic until exposed to the air and rain. But there is a lot that we still do not know about the effects of toxins in the food chain.

Stocks of toxins

Huge amounts of toxins will enter the food chain simply because we have great stores of them. We do not know how to get rid of them. Toxic chemicals and radioactive material are stored in thousands of barrels and underground tanks across the world. They enter the food chain mostly through leakage. Containers develop holes and the substances inside ooze out, or they drip through broken pipes. From here, they easily get washed into the food chain.

Toxic seas

The sea contains enormous amounts of toxins, too. We are slowly finding out how these can spread. Studies from Canada's Arctic region show that seabirds called fulmars carry toxins from the fish and dead matter that they eat.

◄ *Industrial incinerator smokestacks release toxic substances into the air.*

The birds release the toxins in droppings miles beneath the cliffs of their nesting sites. There are 20,000 fulmars in the part of Canada that was studied, so that is a lot of toxins.

The wildlife of Costa Rica's tropical forests is being ➤ *affected badly by crop spraying in the lowlands.*

CASE STUDY

Effects of climate change

There are signs that global warming could spread toxins into new environments. In Costa Rica's lowlands, farmers use pesticides and herbicides on their fruit crops. Mostly, these chemicals have not carried far from the fields. But unusually warm weather over the lowlands has concentrated the strength of the toxins in the air. Warm air always rises, and global warming has meant that extra-warm air containing these concentrated toxins has risen even higher. It has reached right up into the previously unspoilt cloud forests of Costa Rica. The cloud forests are now showing signs of toxic poisoning to both plants and animals. The insecticide, endosulfan, and the fungicide, chlorothalonil, have accumulated in the cloud forest ecosystem. These chemicals are poisoning plants and animals, especially amphibians such as frogs.

◀ *Spraying crops may reap short-term rewards, but it may mean long-term damage to the environment.*

Protecting our planet

Governments across the world are trying to ban the use of toxins that harm the food chain. They are working to find solutions to industrial smog and waste sludge that hold toxins. The United Nations Environment Program has pushed forward many projects to stop the production of harmful chemicals.

No simple solutions

Emerging nations, such as China and India, want to make their countries richer through industry. It is very hard for them to control toxins at the same time. Some toxic chemicals have helped humankind enormously, though they are now banned in many countries. For example, **DDT** has helped stop the spread of malaria, dengue fever, and typhoid for nearly 70 years.

"Plans to protect air and water, wilderness and wildlife are in fact plans to protect man."

Stewart Udall, U.S. politician and ecologist

Recycling plastic garbage, ➤ rather than throwing it away, can help reduce the number of toxins that enter the food chain.

28

These killer diseases are carried by mosquitoes which the chemical DDT helps to destroy. Unfortunately, at the moment, there are no better alternatives for countries that really need to stop people from dying or suffering from such diseases.

Growing your own, chemical-free food can help ➤
to reduce the number of toxins in the food chain.

HOW CAN WE PROTECT OUR PLANET?

- Try to use safer cleaning products at home: natural soap made from vegetable oils, lemon juice and vinegar for cleaning surfaces, a drop of olive oil to polish furniture, tea tree oil or eucalyptus oil as natural disinfectants.

- Re-use plastic bags. Take your own bags when you go shopping.

- Try growing your own chemical-free vegetables and herbs. You can grow a lot even in pots on a balcony or in a back yard.

- Consider updating your software first before you decide to buy a new computer. Do not automatically update your old cell phone. Do you really need to?

- Try to use recyclable glass bottles, or look for the recycling logo on your plastic bottles.

- In Australia, bottles are being made of biodegradable corn starch. Some have tree seeds embedded in them. These grow on waste sites as the bottles break down. Trees are really good for the environment as they absorb carbon gases that lead to global warming.

MADE OF 100% RECYCLED PAPER

Glossary

acids Stinging chemicals. Powerful acids are very dangerous

algae Simple plant-like forms that can be tiny or as big as seaweed

amphibians Creatures such as frogs, toads, or newts

crustaceans Animals that are protected by a shell that covers their body

DDT A strong pesticide, full name is dichlorodiphenyltrichloroethane

fungicides Chemicals that kill fungi on crops

groundwater Underground water that is often drawn up from wells

herbicide A chemical weed killer

hormones Chemicals produced by a body or plant. They control many functions, such as reproduction

landfill sites Places where huge amounts of garbage are dumped

leach To transport chemicals into the soil by water

lichens Plant-like growths that are part fungi, part algae

nutrients Chemicals, such as vitamins, that help growth in plants and animals

PCBs Cancer-causing substances used in electrical equipment. Full name is polychlorinated biphenyl

pesticides Chemicals that kill pests such as insects

plankton Tiny plants and animals that live in the ocean

radioactive Containing harmful rays released from certain natural substances such as uranium

radioactive fallout The spread of harmful radioactive rays

reptiles Cold-blooded creatures such as snakes or lizards

sterilized When something is changed so that it is unable to reproduce. Also to clean something very thoroughly so no organisms can live on it

surfactants Chemicals that relax the material being cleaned. This allows the cleaning agent to work properly

waterways Routes through which water runs, such as rivers or streams

Further information

Books

Reducing Your Foodprint: Farming, Cooking, and Eating for a Healthy Planet (Energy Revolution) by Ellen Rodger (Crabtree, 2010)

Growing and Eating Green: Careers in Farming, Producing, and Marketing Food (Green-Collar Careers) by Ruth Owen (Crabtree, 2010)

Food Chains series by Robert Snedden (Franklin Watts, 2009)

Waste and Recycling (Can the Earth Cope?) by Louise Spilsbury (Wayland, 2008)

Web sites

Find out how farming practices are affecting our food chain:
www.olliesworld.com/planet/usa/info/info/sr_ag03.htm

Click on the "Children and Youth" section to discover how you can help to care for the environment at:
www.unep.org

Learn more about the huge problem of plastic pollution, especially water bottles at:
www.kids.nationalgeographic.com/Stories/SpaceScience/Water-bottle-pollution

Index